A SWALE A
SORT OF SWADDLE

ABBY WALTHAUSEN

SPUYTEN DUYVIL
New York City

ISBN 978-1-963908-61-9

Library of Congress Control Number: 2025931551

... streams are meeting here that ought to churn up some exciting whirlpools.

— James M. Cain, "Paradise"

...and your bald cry
Took its place among the elements.

— Sylvia Plath, "Morning Song"

Contents

ONCE AROUND

The Zeroes taught
    Us – Phosphorous –
We learned to like the Fire
By handling Glaciers – when a
    Boy –
And Tinder – guessed – by power

Of Opposite – to equal Ought –
Eclipses – Suns – imply –
Paralysis – our Primer dumb
Unto Vitality –

      —Emily Dickinson, 284

RELIQUARY #1

In this manila pocket I have placed

sand caked together with zinc
from your first visit to the beach

clipped nails, a cowlick hardened
clipped hair, a crescent limp

and the meteor your navel brought,
a little oxblood stone.

Shocking, all this sloughing, so soon —
though when we stand still
we see these tidbits shed
to honor growth.

DOCKING

Puffed up and a week late
you were suspended and hard to coax
like me in an adopted city, never close
to the ocean as the palms showed,
so bobbing in an inland pool.

And I didn't know the names of plants here
except for those I'd known on sills — jade and pencil —
here monstrous enough to fill
yards and yard scrap bins:
abundance
and ignorance,
no name yet.

The doctors sought the unnamed too — one said *the za is done*
but I'd been settling in this sprawling patchwork, so I knew it was *the concha*
that was done and pink
and crackling
yet unwilling, I got it, the way we both dissociated —
        as though competing for the role
(I know, I did not invent this) of Dr. Caligari's somnambulist —
and when you won — resisting all inductions —
they tucked in and they went gorey
and we were glad we'd named you valiantly, victor full of fricative sounds
because, again, the rush:

not one single photo from these bursts
captured a salty scream or your big hands shaking
like some little crust picked from a tide pool
and dropped a few crags from home.

Gruesome, we know, but fortune
has your folding mind showing soon
how those hands belong to you.

FLYBY

Life is long but can be thicker when I try
I am happy, but can only live one strand at a time.

Pluto's huge valentine showed us no life
and since still water is still poor viewing,
we watched *The Wrong Man*, Hitchcock's plainest,
hoping to find an unseen eddy there.

Old quips get lost in the dishwater
of one long and glowing noir.
Westerns too dissolve their crackling filaments
and constellations shed their nets and names.

But now night and day are the same frontier,
chaperoned by light as dim as dimmest screen,
ragbag now presents a roll, a kick, a muscle, a curl.

And someday, maybe a word.

This just new! Life's labor
to sift and save a few.

Substantial Haunting

(and what pregnancy isn't queer? an open question.)

1.
Lived before the mirror,
what I presumed the trailhead
of abstraction
in its burrow.

Storm clouds at midday trigger
the street lights and headlights and
clap at the back alley motion sensors.

A hazy sound photo to find
out that I embody on
my own, typically,
hetero.

Rare-unknown-ditto, mounded up,
crumbs to follow
filling up.
I quickly dropped my gathered shirt hem
when someone quick was looking.

2.
One year later, a pulled muscle brings
back the twitch of quickening.
Like riding a bicycle?
To find life winding up inside.
To skip the scores of symptoms?

The phantom starts beheading.
No — starts swapping heads.

In Limbo

The marriage, the womb,
Houses of privacy and relax
"What news?" the catholic generations asked.

I said family drive was missing, replaced
by ethics and a question
and I wouldn't stop to think about stopping an accident.

Then a quake whose fault was not of dogmas
or sentiments but of the purely furred
urge to bound forward.

To learn about an extra finger,
growing out of nowhere, by unseen pollination,
why rush to cut it off?

So curiosity's what's likable about
the holy mary and her spouse?

Awkward and shadow-warping
but after birth, that grand pax of beauty
to watch all this fleshy excess
find its use.

And how many uses can there
be for parts of an entire being?

Dark horse cures to hope for, hope in escrow,
as the concept of planning
drowns in determination
to replicate appendage, the self to scale
with thumb on the scale.

Low Tides

The neck loosens and leaves
the head filling out like a waxing moon,
and skull still sessile rises on its column.

A bone has obligations
and a rattle holds the sound of tiny chaos
and acceptance that all events
happen once, at once,
without the honk of tidings.

The conchs baked in the sun,
which called shells sundials,
and called you and me sundials too,
and it was our breath that made
whorls squawk, real and sound and spitty.

Functionally, you do not hear the ocean there,
it's all echoes of erosion, of tidal critter dried
without the life buffer,
without those melding butters.

SEA-RING

Four plastic creatures,
invertebrate and spiny mixed,
gathered on a ring.

Loves variations on a key
or set of them.

Quarterly and taxonomic,
teasing your fresh immunities,
a shining new set
of vaccines.

2016 / 1984

and motherhood is not a home you live in
but a warren of beautiful rooms… like the Alhambra
on a winter morning, some well-trod but magnificent place
you're only allowed to sit in for a minute

Granted, the millenia skipped over
on a date like any other, and it hits me that today
I teeter past the mirrored silhouettes
that my own birth year
cut and claimed
in the fat silly shadow of y2k.

Anachronism was popular
with historic-mansion-californians who
built fresh estates of far flung rocks and gathered them into
a faultline
of centuries and plates, with old parquets and new archness.
And that is how the robber barons robbed time
and gilded it…
My only wish!

Steady, for this moment, orange grove
and railroad, turret and
sixteen twice and finally even-tempered
between two human eras. Poised!
for a third ascent to adolescence
on this my thirty-second birthday.

What a time to place a lintel,
what a time to call cleft, above the cradle
which uses equilibrium to soothe,
moored, nod nod, to each corner of the room.

This new foundation lies above the basement.
I live up with a child now, mess of moons and mezzalunas,
his monument a date
outgrown and dipped in bronze
like any other.

ALL FORTIFIED

Your feet make an illogical headstand,
but so do mine.
What a sagging ramrod, the spine.

Our neighborhood's an envelope
with cypress fringed limits.
Hikes are less buoyant wrapped in great canvas
pocket, sweat and hot breath and backs
hunched like parenthesis.

Sturdy joints
will move you soon and so will
solid foods.

Bones can grow but teeth keep their rows
and replace. Nothing integral,
just a first line utensil.

ARID LAND

A swale, one way
to quiet water.
A swale, a sort of swaddle.

On this trail,
each step a landslide, an hourglass
without its narrowing channel.

On this trail, so heavy in a sling:

On this attachment
I hang the philosophical
and practical.

My baby ought
for now (brush fires high)
to stay portable.

Bag of Waters

Translucence, I hear, was one of
your first qualities
but that was before there was any
light to inspect you against.

We posed you like a houseplant, near the window,
to cure the yellow of your first weeks out.

We are both water mostly then and now,
blue surface, reflective,
like anyone in a crowd.

I hear that human lake whenever
hiccups overlap with laughs:
they're fully round and eerie,
clarifying nothing.

Aerial Roots

Left in the garden, would you subsist
on ficus berries, those private fruits,
neutral egg, double dome, dense seed
without the meat?

"City beautiful" placed those trees with a master plan:
Shade and shelter!
But ninety year roots have made a hash of sidewalks
and buried breadcrumbs and tectonic trails
alike in wild ball bearings.

Our ¾ apartment, tucked away,
and hinges painted shut with suspect, leady paint
and the slow leak of the stove
and the off-gas of the memory foam,
that springless trampoline.

Inside, outside, little risks
on mother's rest and restlessness:
to hang a swing, inflate a tire?

The wheel was at first a plaything if
its prototype appeared from food.
Test it.
The toy is the most rugged tool.

On an Airplane

Carried in a cab there, and carried again
through mechanical geologists
that find no fillings and buckles on you.

Carried in the dreamliner, auk and eider,
with hundreds cozy in the most efficient car,
modern wonder with ancient pack to lurch and soar.

Between all the journey's wooly legs
is the quiet moment I release you to your hands and knees —
a deceptive visit to the ground
where you steer tiny cars of ore
with your own rubber palms.

Energy in, energy out,
the missing passport stamp —
the lap to hold this year, this date
—is still of real import.

Icon Blooms

Baby of the lake, flowering
with petals savory like shallots, purple
blush suggesting, not emitting,
sharp perfume.

We entered as tourists the parsonage but never the temple of Miss Missing
Aimee Semple who was the evangelist preferred by Monroe and Chaplin both
— and somehow my sense of campiness decamped — I mean the woman
kidnapped herself — and I fell complicit with the docent to ignore what's
infamous and to agree — agree about her grace her innocence and the pleats
of her evening dress.

Often these days, stunted by the onset of unexpected reverence.

Here in Echo Park you have heard recorded church bells
still atmosphere in desert air
and on our travels "east" but west of here,
you felt the felty twitch
of a gong hit and left to rest.

We poured tea on the infant Buddha as is custom for that nativity, which we
learned is called Matsuri, but your hands splashed in the basin, grabbing
for the mellow icon — lookouts, us, bending rules with all respect, visiting
tradition — even with sticky fingers you are pure spring and every brush
with water is a ritual ablution.

Often these days, a sudden rush of porousness.

In mud seasons, a flower frog, a honeycomb
of woody winter chambers.

You yawned through your year,
our travels,
and once again the lotus surfaced
and opened up its daybook.

VINES AND BINES

Hid by the august foliage and fruit of the grape-vine
twine
your anatomy
round the pruned and polished stem,
Chameleon.
Fire laid upon
an emerald as long as
the Dark King's massy
one,
could not snap the spectrum up for food as you have done.

— Marianne Moore, "To a Chameleon"

RELIQUARY #2

I tuck lavender and rosemary
around the !ap neck of your shirt
and in my sleeve

I save those sprigs for this manila pocket.

The wafting scent will fade but the oils
will cloister for another year—
resin for all time
resin without pine
how strange that your first evergreens
have so little, weather-wise, to withstand.

Vernaculars

Newer than religion, and green
and squeezed, between
scientologists and rosicrucians,
bathed only in the light of the hollyhock,
of the mission's crystal bells.

Who's to say what's battiest?

The alligator-pear-skin,
not the glass jar, was the vessel of
your first bites.

Symbols stand alone and proud
before the glue of story.

When egg simmers in bonito broth,
we feed you with two bamboo tines.

Food and spirit together
in you and here in the city of irrigation, no need
we hope for gowns and the runoff of initiation.

Mycorrhiza

The richness of those roots
impressed me lacey, the strength
of the forest to send nourishment,
to send warning —
first the seedlings,
then the young protect the old.

You provide the spitty message
and my milk responds in kind
with antibodies and a frothy conversation,
trailing off each day...

I would like to thank that fungus!
But what I ask, will be that fungus when roots
are courteous of each other's space
and deep and dark they don't quite speak?

One day language, great byproduct of saliva
will be my only fungus, my hope
to carry those essential signals.
Deprivation and danger are always electrical,
but other messages?

Your bellybutton is here

To get what you want say please

I'll tell you the signs of a fairweather friend

I don't want to have to scream these
—toyon, oak, and sycamore —
the air of all these trees
arrives to shoulder words.

Fall Customs

The chinese flame tree knows its colors well
enough to mimic autumn where the short
days keep the heat —
singed salmon lanterns detach on election day

as though the climate here in California were in line
with the broader country's
electorate, hectorate, hecate, calexit.

My senators understand me,
educated in the coastal climes of history.

My petitions belong where there aren't any estuaries
and I try cold calls, postcards, and pleas
to replicate my thoughts
in the unfathomable
void of my experience.

The summer is over and for the inland world new affront —
nightsoil from the city arrives and proclaims
One great way to variegated,
heirlooming nightshades.

ACQUISITION

I run a tally of the words you added
but as experiment, it crumbles
with what I missed or you mumbled.

I think a keekoo is a pinecone,
which it may be,
but what is this bottle brush of seeds to you?

Verlan of a cookie
was the solution I discovered weeks later.

There are grandparents who name themselves
and coach and those who wait and hope
for a few nice syllables, tailored, their own.

The baby is plenty poet from now on,
but doesn't now — he never will —
make commissioned words.

Slow Abscission

A full word is far and away
the most complicated shape.
You will recognize one maybe sometime after
Squash & Circle, then Square

& Serif,
the callous the succulent cutting needs
before contact with the soil,
before rooting,
the rough
to keep from rotting.

Pothos is my best old script,
winding around the dotted lines of grammar / grade.

From now on, no babble of sentence
is ever again so bramble-connected.

INSTRUCTION

New habit: to speak
directions loud and clear

to an intense and mostly
silent audience
and to overspeak procedures.

For enrichment: piano variations
to complicate the silences.
I dictate the details of hinges. Gate and cupboard,
I echo from the mailbox and the oven.

Don't pinch yourself!
Hold the rail because…
wending here are passion fruits,
who need, according to the grocer,
loose trellis and
positive emotional climate
to flower and to thrive.

Confirmed — I'm talking in the right direction —
a lot of little notes and words make passion.

Vines and Bines

This year Leo and Felix are the names,
August, hot and feline.
But if that Santa Ana had blown
damper, brought my alternates
list, the crew called Sylvan
and Linnaeus?

A Poppy is your first peer at birth,
making 10 weeks more noises
10 weeks less wobble around the neck
and later, words, solutions.

At a year and a half, you look at each
other to laugh, before that only to push
with whatever limbs worked best.

At a year and a half, your hair
has long pieces that take on every texture,
and comb or no, remain separate tendrils.

At a year and a half, you took
the world's lead and called out
the sappy appellation — mommy —
but on days we stay housebound
you forget influence beyond
those winding first syllables, so back
you thread through ma and mas and mama.

MEDIAN STRIP

Head, head holder,
knees and toes.

The cypress sends its periscope of wood —
the oak below the waterline is cork.

Eyes, hear near,
and mouth and nose.

The countertop potato is a shame —
a new one in the neighborhood
to see the lazy parking job I've done.

A new tree, such an event
when its purpose is to divide
and direct traffic.

Branch and trunk and locked up cone —
a system self-contained under
leafy breathing clothes.

Water Management

Street trees —
a forest of strangers
complicit nonetheless
as sponges.

False lake —
some valley towns
preserved against coming,
crumbling heat-age.

Some valley towns
gone to lakeweed.

Some valley towns
renamed by fathom number
and blue shade.

Asphalt —
catchment suppressed,
rain too fast over it.

NATIVE RESEEDINGS

Here the hummingbird
drinks
like a maraschino cherry.

Do we sound critical
when we walk the neighborhood for nature?

Here the gopher
tosses
up a hundred clever pedestals
to celebrate his sated face.

Who is the keystone species here?

We linger at the entropic playground, vacant corner
where the neighborhood outgrows its toys
and someone tends a kumquat.

Even jasmine's thick velvet lash,
scratches the surface of the desert all around it.
So we inhale it's heady criticism
and praise
pious buckwheat, planned and planted
to bloom in rust
and conquer thirst.

No Gambol

The president used to walk the rose garden
thinking, bending knees.
Now a stranger power hides
in the hedges, a barrier gnarly
for its reach.

It hides in hedges
and imitates a bird frustrated
by half of its own feathers.

I think it seems likely mostly
certain
that the best marbled hybrid,
a yellow with coral tips and stripes of pink
should belong only
to overbooked bees and worried
over by one born at this moment:

that baby has the most to lose,
the longest time a button away.
Fuck the rose, in any case,
clipped back to nothing
and blooming to applaud abuse!

Westways has Suggestions

1. Nordhoff becomes Ojai

"The Moon" in Chumash
makes a better valley for tourism
than unresolved
war problems.

Milder than teutonic,
underneath the hills —
Mayor Moon would suggest
lemon, orange, pomelo
for Health, Pleasure,
and Residence.

That pickled astrologer,
he's full of windchimes
and he winds vacations to an end
just to predict next
getaways

and he keeps the local high school Nordhoff
as it's compulsory,
a secular welcome-rug-gag,
sweet trapdoor
of "the Nest."

2. WRIGHTWOOD, TWO ELEVATIONS

The snow on chaparral
is a pastel thing —
sage scented ice
brightens the stark and white
of snow on bare trees.

Those batwings live in the terrace-toned valley
where fire last season cleared the sand
and charred old trunks
of cacti playing tree.
Contained burn, like the sun
and the striking lines of sunset served all day.

The diner in town
has one menu only
for two sides of the treeline,
costs every broken shard of sled the hikers find.
All people, all tubers, all times of day:
Thirsty and their
appetite all alpine.

Too Much

The neighborhood is overloaded with old names
that need all the dusting of a botanic garden.
Edendale,
Elysian Heights,
Echo Park,
even Dodgertown is lovely when
the people of Chavez Ravine stay on to judge it.
Their breath is the thin air of the upper deck;
they weigh a game, a blanched skyline,
black palms, heat columns the ravens ride.

If the wild west was shaped by Hollywood,
the coastal sky was shaped by nothing —
the empty blue breaks only for drab scrub of mountains,
National forest textured, from this distance,
more like dry tastebud than like greenlung.

A cloud passes over the terrain, is no developer
and stays rich with cubic footage, inside, out,
itching like a bulbous pearl.

I have seen freshwaters laid
in fine jewelry as Neptune's rippling torso.
I would use such a dud gem to correct a clear day
or as a dice for choosing
a clammy, dimpled toddler's stagename.

VESSELS FOR /
WEANING WITH

Something about mothers
>*A List*
>>>*I need to go to the health food store*
To get a bottle of milk and a piece of Laughing Grasshopper tofu
You think something like a book will change the world, don't you?
I do, I take pleasure in taking the milk with the most cream
But I don't understand why we have to be repeaters like criminals
The bread at the bakery is lively, expensive and pretentiously thick
My mother's mother was a stocky solid woman who rewarded us
With intense glances through her spectacles and miniscule tips,
My mother had a sharp intelligence denuded by religion and remorse,

— Bernadette Mayer, from *Midwinter Day*

RELIQUARY #3

In this manila pocket I have placed

photos of you drinking deeply
from three favorite cups,
since I have no tools
for archiving flavors.

I can only really watch you when you feed.
Pained and focused, on your inside eyelids,
the novel and invented shapes of all the lactose
nuance you first taste.

The watering cups are cute
but I have been groundwaters.
I have been the conduit of curry powders,
watermelon, crisped-up greens
and that exchange is so opaque
to me.

I.   LEARNER CUP

Tusks bring ceremony
and a forceful, ever-ready spout.

Do not chastise this chalice,
you buck-toothed friends of dentists.

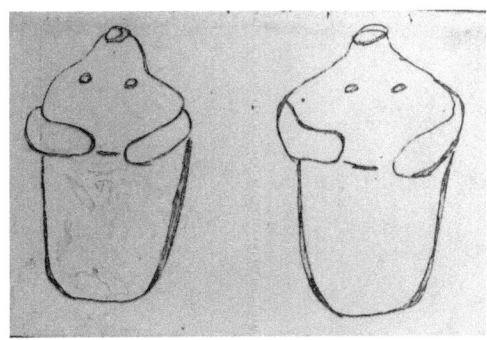

II.   PUP CUP

Animation of stone fetish,
wink of turquoise toy.

The worldly liver rests in clay, hyena head.
The heart, pharaoh's headdress always,
cools unwillingly in jet.

III.   MIRACLE CUP

The drain is a kinetic pendant;
the amphora is the vessel to drain.

Under the grapevine, under leaves,
pressing out the skins and the seeds,
snails study ways of easy winding.

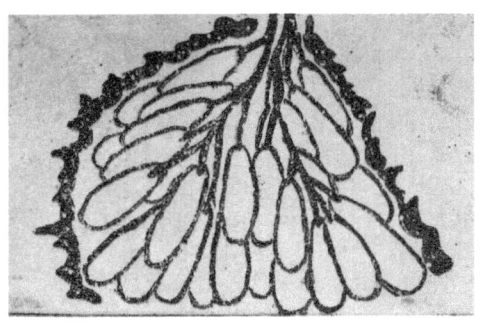

IV.   Galactophore, Engorged

At the museum now I get
the goddesses with tight high stone breasts
poised to pour forth at a mewl.

This one has an arm for every baby
passing through this morning
but just the typical emergency of tits.

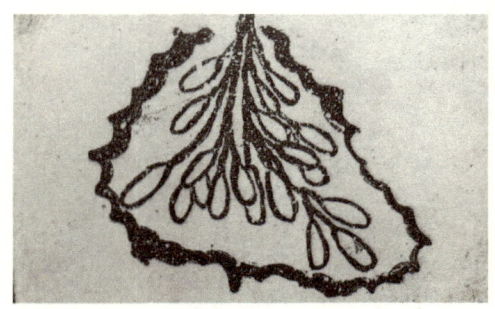

V. GALACTOPHORE, LOOSE

Sad as famous piety
is the milky mary healing eyes.

Just conjunctivitis... and the baby?
Nurseryside, with busy mother now disjoined.

REHOMING

Winter and summer till old age began
My circus animals were all on show,
Those stilted boys, that burnished chariot,
Lion and woman and the Lord knows what.

—W. B. Yeats, "The Circus Animals' Desertion"

Reliquary #4

In this manila pocket I have placed
the dog-ears overcreased, fallen from your books,
a pop-up bear torn from
another story.

Zoo Drive connects two zoos,
one gone to seed, one new.

The drive is short between
lions sedated in the summer heat
and lions dispersed by time.

The small abandoned cages don't cramp
your imagination —
they are a stage to play the forefathers,
fiercer,
than the ones down the road
lolling in the shade.

Most animals you've met are bright and eager
to bring you a message from the page.
They are realer than the zoo, than the wild.
They wear their little pants and they speak your language
— sentences of it — eons before you do.

Morals

What comets can I offer
without Joseph-doula
and sheep-wives and cow-wives
and a baby-god flat-packed in hay?

A range of applied pieties —
against pan proteins,
for storybook farmers,
for the icecaps of the earth,
against a token virus —
energies most adamant
against the slice of Candlemas —
for open-sourced, expansive otherness.

Once while picnicking at a random mothers gathering —
which seemed at first anachronistic — I spaced out and you crawled
off to palm a goose turd — and as you brought it to your mouth I
grabbed you fast by the overalls, I jerked your hand and scrubbing it,
warned the mothers of younger ones — the wolves be in mobility —
gasps — not for the bomb of pathogens but for my bruteness of my grasp —
oh no! to lifting from behind — much less without permission —

Gentle parents, please,
It's weird for me to worship baby
when baby and I together — keep dirt as deity and devil —
clean paws over here — amending soil over there —

All crud, rind, and core to destiny,
in the harmony plot of composting.

Better story, descend on values!
Oh, to transubstantiate
or at least explode
a better blend of logic and anecdote.

While the Pepper Lasts

The bear is proud of his new crown 'I'm the king of the forest.'
He is not the only one who has changed but...achoo.

A force of change inspired in unsettled dust.
Original sin comes out a bit each time,
to be replaced with something more contrived.

I heard the number of colds is finite —
mutations can't compete with magic numbers —
but are the years that follow ones of good health
or a full stop, when sick and well are both fully dealt?

A helicopter, tight pendulum on an upturned wheel
shushes and pulses above a deadlocked grid.
You say *ha copa copa* and point
at it landing on a lauded children's hospital.
Ha copa copa and my eyes blur and systems still
for the critical moment I know plays out
in the cabin of a carnival ride.

You leave matter everywhere;
but do you matter everywhere?
both I fear is helpful
for hexers.

THE DOCUMENT SAFE

Observe sign-posts and milestones;
do not gobble herring bones—

Flood might send us to the roof
and discord to a cave of cans.
Busybodies who know have mapped
and claimed the high-rent moon.

Earthly context is a lot here
but there are a few ways you mesh
into this dubious fabric
for now while we know
nothing of your grit—

We know that you are born as per your date and documents
a ram and a ruby, a cancer and a kaiser, a nenuphar and an Obama baby —
grand list to use for speculation while you hide your quirks in sleep.

You are also half Canadian, phew.

For now we are your leader and
you are a citizen of blanket nests and —
seers, we simply won't assume.

The seismometer sees too:
swaddle your house of wood and plaster
in outsized sheets of latex and leather.

Convention 2016

"Likes parades, does he,"
said the President. "Is there any reason,"
the president asked the two aides,
"why we should be going in that direction
rather than this direction?"

That permanent shrug I did not like
in spite of all the optimism —
I know it cradled passively the interests of gunmen.

I thought that he would lose! Hindsight,
so now I know who lost, we lost!

All these square candidates —
not unhip, but neck shrinking towards shoulders,
and crown towards brow.

She had that quality in spades, the reason
people loved her drawn
in any little cube with bars.

He kvetches, she cackles.
Folkloric, almost powerful
step-parents for the masses.

Who is best to stand against the worst?
Everyone will sooner, later be endorsed by spouse.

She folded work into life and he,
affectionate sigh, never thought to fold
those shirts whose labels roughly read
"passionate asceticism."

Young newlywed neighbor, mournfully says:
I would have got pregnant under either of *them*.

Rise Time

*Pete can't answer
because he's only some dough and stuff.*

Handprints for official reasons first,
later for the seasonal and sentimental.

The beautiful cast came out like a cracker
sugar crust on salt dough
for a tree sustained by a liter a day.

Bougainvillea doesn't stop for winter here
and when we pass one.
 it's time to gather blooms to deck the dog leash and our
home.
Hearth tending doesn't stop for spring here either.

My proofing doll will talk someday
and his ideas won't be mine.
Today he picked a grape leaf for the chickens
Today he fanned the floor with a broomish tool
Today he pushed the dog from my lap —
if it was to protest the warm pulse of fur,
already this was an unseasonal idea.

Impudent Puppy

Don't ever ever dig holes under this fence.

1.
Skylla, with purported yapping
was called a puppy so literally
that lure
not of appeal —
we did not always love puppies.

So here I am searching —
duel-who-called-whom-puppy
and finding that that sweetness of ours
launched more fights than just the famous
Hamiltons and Burrs.

Puppies and Babies, an artpiece
puppies and babies, our artpiece
in this age when the serious reject figures.

But come on, a puppy is adoring
and abrasive and a concept and
what is a baby but a minimalist
portrait of the artist?

2.
I have the round face
and soft voice
that strangers call sweetheart.

The fancier flowers have fewer
axes of symmetry.
They are bearded like an uncleaned mussel.

Rules for nature, art, and value
I estimate and write
so long as no one hassles down to me
from behind the keeper's counter.

How many yaps in the black eyed susan?
So much stamina in the daisy's cushion!

What I crave is another baby —
Await my cult
of faces.

As the Crow Flies

And sometimes sent my ships in fleets
All up and down among the sheets;
Or brought my trees and houses out,
And planted cities all about.

Quilts these days are made
of piecework made for quilting —

washed fields of counterpane and framer's
craquelure only sometimes come with age.

All of this acceleration and its opposite!
Security may learn someday to rummage
my suitcase at the rate the plane flies.

A route is so quick to procure,
but takes as long as ever
for aesthetes like us
to pace and learn.

SPRING POSITIONING

"Sweetness, sweetness, sweetness," murmured
the mouse, and she ate him up entirely.

Ducklings, goslings,
gold monstrance of plush infancy,
tufted and adored on shelling —
what of little grebes and loons?

All eat the froglings before leg-time,
jeweled favors like the nascent things
in league with yolk and sprout and veal.

Saplings flow with sugars
of the easter basket
but plan their skirts of interference
between the green and grass.

The shadow is born with its host
and coots harass until dead
the hatchling who begs the hardest.

The pond waters are are mottled treat —
mirror and algae —
and both nourish plenty
from what we at the surface can see.

DESKILLING

The animals that were ...
the animals that are ...
and the animals that will be...

In the cave of his worry-cleft skull,
the old creature spent his final year.
You almost learned to speak his name.

Were his cataracts full of floaters?
Not a small distraction from plain sight
but bold against white, glyphs
sliding by like herds of cinder fleas.

Those are the scratches you learn before
your phonemes and perspective.
They are bound together. And to haunt you later.

The poor dog we bound in our unfocused grief —
I read "Death of a Pig" like I did for the dog before.

And as an artifact
I saved the cartouche of our family name,
bearing all contact — number, word.

Learned not Trained

Stanley had a secret trick so he could stay outside.
When he was out and had to go, Stanley liked to hide.

At some point I wonder
if you sleep so well because of all
the wine I drink.

A security guard somewhere told me I could
oil and press your head
into shape.

I know that hope-cum-fidget,
worrying my square front teeth
back into their arched template.

I will be vigilant about the changing of shoe size
so you can grow those toes aligned!

Another mother insists
it's *potty learned* not *potty trained* —
so what then do Olympians get up to
with their compacted loops?
Muscles and their limits
from now on will keep you tethered
to restroom.

You leaf through your books, pre-reader that you are,
like a sentient storm.

What virtues are my fault
and which aren't?

Stepping Up

Take good care of the baby, Carl.

The young dog, in spite of early spaying,
was activated by the milk that sprayed
in every corner of the apartment.

She wanted to adopt you and grab you
by the neck wrinkle, and teach you how to choose a
nipple
and when she found you swaddled and stashed
out of reach
she rolled up her pillow, her pleasure,
some plot to conceive.

Did she know she was demoted?
Along with the calendar, newsfeed,
stick of incense, shift of sun?

Sure once in a while I know the year still,
but with this little dog goes the whole right world:

I hate he who took "dopey"
and spoiled that sweet scold!

I hate that my failure to engage
is now so raw, limp, exposed!

I resolve this year that infancy's unbroken
chain of photos will include that lonesome pet,
the mirror;
That the baby must hold in every shot
a daily, dated paper.

Springing Off

They would never, never again sharpen their teeth
on the rope that held them so safely to shore.

A primitive "don't bite the hand" —
indeed a rope not only fed you,
but held you where no hands could reach.

To look you in the mouth, to date those stones of flesh,
I have to make you laugh…
a simple task with props.
Every volume of your alphabets,
just for sound, includes some wild irrelevance
like the mandatory X-ray transparency.

And yaks? Why yaks?
To read and keep jaws jabbing
with gift-horse-gifts
on full display.

We live country mornings, coyotes
on housecats on chickens on the dusty trail.
We live city afternoons, past grill carts and vendors
where pigeons stop off.

Kernels, husks, and processed crumbs
surround the citadel of children.
Almost every day some bigger child adopts your curls.
They are sweet,
but I step in — they may be wolves
and I, with my succor, am surely a she-wolf —
eternally your she-wolf.

Measure H

The movers said, "Sure, this house is as good as ever.
She's built so well we could move her anywhere."
So they jacked up the little house and put her on wheels.

I narrowed, but this happy narrowing
was that much more for
bubbling over:

I rub those riverstones
in notebooks and in cooking food,
in tending herb pots, laundering,
all private tending.

I tumble the newscycle with insouciance,
and buff the doorknob with soft cloth,
but you turn it once and wander wide.

The temperature is mild, but other things
about the air are harsh:

If you could choose a home it
might be the Dash bus,
wending a local route.

I would live there with you
to avoid discussion
of stucco and cardboard, overflowing
with stigmas and the dumbest luck.

DRIVERLESS TRAFFIC

Trucks as far as eyes can see...which truck would you like to be?

By 2030, I expect the death of contact
sports and cars that need
your innocence in the driver's seat.

I mean, we read about purpose-driven
cars each day and spread the covers flat,
your library laid edge to spine
to pave the room
for good little cars to act.

Your toys, they work fine full or empty.
Who's driving, you ask?
No people — choking hazards as well
as hazards of projection.

A friend of mine, when you were bored at dinner
taught you "crash"
now you say it from the backseat
while I drive.

Your father taught you to — help! — undo
your safety belt
now I think about that looseness
while I drive.

DIRECTIONS

"If you become a little boy and run into a house," said the mother bunny,
   "I will become your mother and catch you in my arms and hug you."

1.
Choo-choo-one-nine Echo Park Avenue,
the gate, the mailbox,
the left up our street.
Will you mnemonic for a cop, if you're ever lost?

We have been here two years, a long time
in this touch tank of pets and plants —
we brush past hearty little succulents
that don't need much room.

I'd like you like a stonecrop, stray a little but
on your own, not on some hiker's boot.
Or like a barnacle that doesn't bother.

A native state with a camino,
a native city with tar bubbling through,
the raw materials for roads,
but will you pave and take them?

2.
A cherry-red matchbox,
a talisman, a worry stone,
a vote of confidence
in this town.

At the museum,
a patchy-bald pile of pelts and claws.
Visitors did that shiny left breast to Alma Mater
and polished right foot to founding father,
random tributes to the hand we are the first to use.

Sea Snails and conchs and their lookalike sweets
inherit their twirling chiralities.
The hermit trimester could pass in any of these, but
you walk now and when you move away, you must choose
a place with room for rocks, sticks, books
and other relics of these days
or at least a fire stair that's going your way!

Notes

The epigraph in "Substantial Haunting" comes from Maggie Nelson's introduction to A.L. Steiner's zine *Puppies and Babies*. The epigraph in "2016 / 1984" comes from Lydia Kiesling's novel *The Golden State*.

With gratitude to the weird riches of children's literature, I took the fragments in the "Rehoming" section from the following books:

"Morals," Maurice Sendak's *Pierre*

"While the Paper Lasts," Virginie Morgand's *Achoo!*

"The Document Safe," Beatrix Potter's *The Tale of Pigling Bland*

"Convention 2016," Lore Segal's *Tell Me a Mitzi*

"Rise Time," William Steig's *Pete's a Pizza*

"Impudent Puppy," Janette Sebring Lowrey's *The Pokey Little Puppy*

"As the Crow Flies," Robert Louis Stevenson's "The Land of Counterpane"

"Spring Positioning," Russell Hoban's *The Marzipan Pig*

"Deskilling," Alice and Martin Provensen's *Our Animal Friends at Maple Hill Farm*

"Learned not Trained," Hope Vestergaard's *Potty Animals*

"Stepping Up," Alexandra Day's *Good Dog Carl*

"Springing Off," George Duplaix's *The Merry Shipwreck*

"Measure H" Virginia Lee Burton's *The Little House*

"Driverless Traffic," Hope Vestergaard's *Digger, Dozer, Dumper*

"Directions," Margaret Wise Brown's *The Runaway Bunny*

ACKNOWLEDGEMENTS

"Morals" appeared in *Mer Vox*, January 2019

"Learned not Trained" appeared in *Foundry*, December 2017

Thank you to Alex who always supported me as I Magoo'ed my way into blessings upon blessings and Bartleby'ed my way into the life of a writer.

Thank you to John, expert-vaunted-musicologist-level brother and uncle.

Thank you to my parents who read me *Runaway Bunny* and taught me to scrutinize each word.

Thank you to my friends who have read and brought fresh eyes to my work and who talk with me and open my eyes to new exciting art, literature, and film every day.

Thank you to Martin who, thanks to forest school, knows the contours of the neighborhood better than any of us now.

Thank you most of all to Henry, the artist and creator of "Cherry Red," the big poet, the famous driver, and the green belt who moves me everyday and has inspired this work of many years.

Abby Walthausen is a writer and teacher living in Los Angeles.